Start to
Felt...

Ewa Kuniczak

SEARCH PRESS

First published in Great Britain 2008
Search Press Ltd
Wellwood
North Farm Road
Tunbridge Wells
Kent TN2 3DR

Text copyright © Ewa Kuniczak 2008

Photographs by Roddy Paine Photographic Studios

Photographs and design copyright © Search Press Ltd.
2008

ISBN-13: 978-1-84448-262-7

Suppliers
If you have difficulty obtaining any of the materials
and equipment mentioned in this book, please visit the
Search Press website for details of suppliers:
www.searchpress.com

Dedicated to Megan

Acknowledgements

Heart-felt thanks to Edd Ralph and Roz Dace, my

editors at Search Press, for making this book possible,

and to Khalzan Dorjkhand, of the 'Duuren Sanaa', the

Mongolian Craft Foundation, for the Mongolian felt

image used on page 4.

The publishers would like to thank consultant
Rebecca Vickers and also the following for appearing in
the photographs: Ellie and Catriona Outram,
Henrietta Amos, Josie Paine, Beth Miller, Jade Searles,
Joelle Nicholson, Charlotte Brooks, Phoebe Cheong
and Lucia Brisefer.

Some words are underlined <u>like this</u>. They are
explained in the glossary on page 48.

Printed in Malaysia

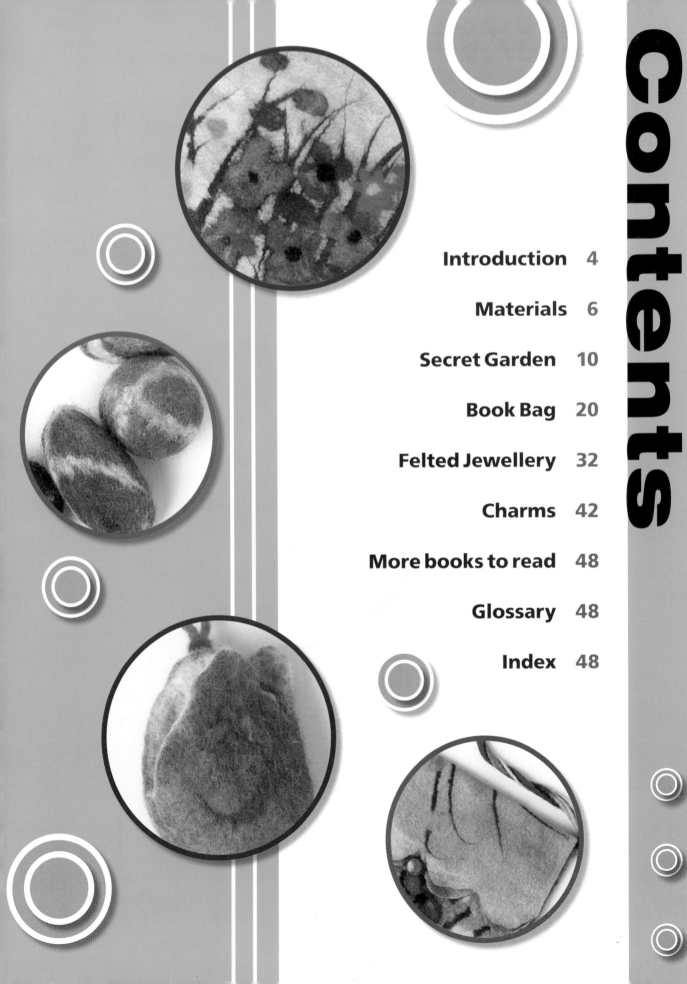

Contents

Introduction 4

Materials 6

Secret Garden 10

Book Bag 20

Felted Jewellery 32

Charms 42

More books to read 48

Glossary 48

Index 48

Introduction

Feltmaking is probably the oldest textile craft in the world. It is amazing how a pile of fluffy wool can be transformed into a fabric that can withstand wind, rain, and fire! It is quite magical, and happens when woollen fibres are moist, warm, and rubbed together.

No one really knows where feltmaking was first developed, or how it came about. What we do know is that felting had reached sophisticated levels by 2,500BC, and that travellers lined their boots by wrapping wool around their feet and legs for comfort. Perhaps that is how the first felts were made?

Traditional wool beating for felt-making in Mongolia, with gers in the background

4

To this day, nomadic peoples throughout Central Asia, from Turkey to Mongolia, live in felt tents called *yurts* or *gers*. These are furnished with felt rugs, cushions, mattresses, and even felt cots for babies.

Traditionally, these people also make hats, coats, bags and boots from their sheep's wool.

This book will show you how to felt, with various projects that will help you master basic working methods and give you ideas for future development.

Let your imagination guide you, and enjoy the magic!

Materials

Wool

Handmade felt is made by rubbing wool together with soap and warm water. The scales on the fibres (hairs) tangle together during felting, and create a dense matted material called felt. Wool fibre is measured by <u>Bradford count</u> in the UK and <u>microns</u> elsewhere. Bradford count relates to the spinning length of the fibres, a system that originated in England; whereas the microns measurement is based on the diameter of the fibre (one micron is equal to one millionth of a metre).

The wool can be bought in combed lengths, called <u>tops</u>, from craft shops that stock materials for hand spinning. It can also be bought in craft and fabric stores in bags of wool roving.

Not all wools felt together easily. The coarser the wool, the harder it is to felt, and some (such as Herdwick wool) are almost impossible to felt by hand. Unwashed wool from a sheep's fleece will take longer to felt than the washed tops, because it has a coating of <u>lanolin</u>, which acts like a lubricant and keeps the fibres apart.

Throughout this book, I use 64s (Bradford count) or 20 micron <u>merino</u> wool tops because they felt easily and produce fine quality results.

Avoid buying wool that has been treated with 'super-wash' finish, as this type of wool will not felt at all!

FUNKY FACT

Merino wool will reduce in size by a third to a half during felting.

Conversion table

Bradford	Micron
Finer than 80s	Under 17.7
80s	17.7
70s	19.15
64s	20.6

Decorations

Once you have made a piece of felt, you can decorate it with embellishments like beads, jewellery findings and buttons.

Beads Glass beads are the most effective as they are shiny.

Jewellery findings Findings are brooch backs, fittings for earrings and clasps for necklaces and bracelets.

Stones Even rock and stones can be used with felt to make decorative objects.

Dyes I use all-in-one acid dyes for wool. Pick your own combination of colours!

Needle and thread Use mercerised sewing thread to match your work, and a sewing needle with an eye that you can thread easily. Make sure the needle will go through the holes in the buttons or beads you are using.

Buttons Select ones that will best suit your project.

TOP TIP!

After you have rinsed out all the soap from your felts, always rinse them again in a <u>vinegar rinse</u>, to neutralise the wool, and stop it rotting.

Soap

The other main material we use when making felt is soap. Soap allows the water to penetrate into the fibres, and this enables them to felt together.

Glycerine or olive soap, or any other low-lather soaps are the best to use, as they produce very small bubbles. This means that the woollen fibres remain close together during felting, and therefore tangle together quickly.

Soap solution is made by dissolving the soap in warm water until the water becomes cloudy.

Felting equipment

In addition to wool, soap and embellishments, there are a few other pieces of equipment that you will need to make felt.

- A supply of **hot** and **cold water**.
- A **dry towel** for drying off felts when they are finished.

There are three felting techniques used in this book: flat wet felt rolling, hollow wet felt rolling, and 3D wet felting. Depending on the technique used, you will need some extra items.

Flat wet rolling

Felting mat You can make a felting mat from a 60cm (24in) wide cane window blind, with the fittings removed and threads tied off. These blinds are usually 2m (78¾in) long, and can be cut in half to make two smaller ones.

Nylon net curtain fabric Four pieces of this netting are needed, each the same size as your felting mat. It is called 'sheers fabric' in the US.

10mm (½in) diameter <u>dowelling</u> The dowelling should be the same width as your felting mat.

Sprinkle bottle A sprinkle bottle can be made from a plastic milk bottle, with holes drilled in the lid.

Old towels Two of these are needed for the flat wet rolling method.

Bubble wrap A small piece of bubble wrap is used to help rub more soap into the wool layers without disturbing the surface. Wool will only felt together where it is moist, and this helps the water to penetrate thoroughly.

Iron and ironing board These are used for smoothing out finished felts.

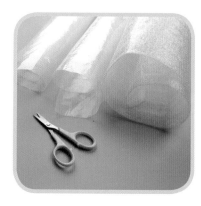

Hollow wet felt rolling

In addition to the items needed for flat wet rolling, you will need:

Clear plastic sheets Two sheets are needed, each the same size as the net curtain pieces.

Piece of heavy-duty plastic 28 x 35.5cm (11 x 14in) This is used for making resist patterns.

Sharp scissors These are used to cut open the felt so that you can remove the heavy-duty plastic when the plastic begins to curl as the woollen layers shrink.

3D wet felting

In addition to the items needed for flat wet rolling, you will need:

Small plastic bowl This is filled with soapy water.

Plastic netting Some fruit and vegetables are wrapped in plastic net, and this sort of netting is ideal for this type of wet felting.

Other equipment

In addition to the main equipment, you will need some other bits and pieces. Most of the equipment can be found in your home, and will not cost much if you need to buy anything you cannot find.

Distilled vinegar This is available in supermarkets. It is acidic, so it counteracts the alkaline soap left in the felt after it is worked.

Large sharp scissors These must be sharp, so be careful.

Clear glue Instant drying clear glue is the best to use.

Tape measure This is used to check the size of the pieces as you felt your work.

Measuring jug This is used to measure the vinegar, water and other liquids used when felting.

Two plastic washing up bowls One bowl is used for rinsing out the soap from the finished felt; and the other is used for the vinegar rinse.

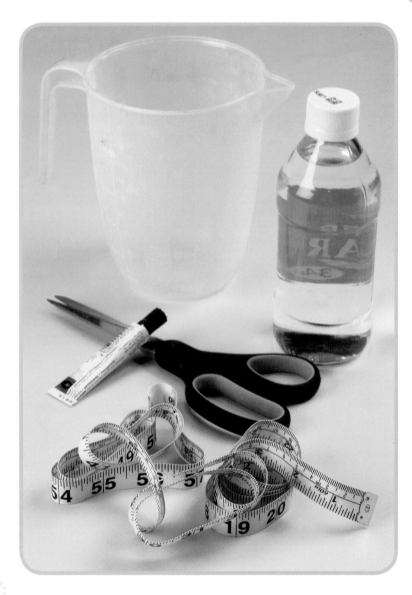

FUNKY FACT

Vinegar rinse is made by adding two tablespoons of clear vinegar to one litre (two US pints) of water.

Secret Garden

In this project you will use the flat wet rolling technique to make the front and back covers of a book. These are decorated with pre-felted shapes. You can make as many inside pages as you like. Making a hidden pocket for holding your secrets will introduce you to using plastic resists.

You will need

Glycerine soap

Measuring jug

White, dark green, light green, light yellow, dark yellow, pink, purple and red merino tops

Equipment for flat wet rolling (see page 8)

Sharp scissors

12.5 x 28cm (5 x 11in) piece of thin plastic for making the resist template for the pocket

Needle and blue thread

Five flower buttons

Vinegar rinse

TOP TIP!

Make sure that you keep your handfuls thin when you pull off the wool from the tops, otherwise your felts will end up thick and clumsy.

1 Dissolve glycerine soap in one litre (two pints) of warm water in your measuring jug to make some cloudy soap solution, then fill your sprinkle bottle.

2 Place the nylon net (sheers fabric) on the felting mat and dampen it with the soap solution.

3 Place handfuls of white merino wool in rows to make an even layer 30 x 32cm (12 x 13in), and sprinkle with soap solution. This is the first layer.

4 For the second layer place handfuls of wool on top at right angles to the previous layer, and sprinkle with soap solution (see inset).

5 Cover with a second net, and pat the surface down with your hands, making sure that all the layers are thoroughly wetted.

6 Sprinkle water on to the bubble side of bubble wrap, and rub extra soap all over it.

7 Turn the bubble wrap over and place it on top of the net. Rub the whole surface, then put the whole piece to one side.

8 We are now going to prepare some pre-felts. Lay out a layer of the dark green tops on a new piece of net (see inset). Sprinkle with soap solution, then add a layer of light green tops at right angles.

FUNKY FACT

Pre-felts are partially felted pieces of wool. You can cut out shapes of them and use them to decorate your background felt.

9 Cover with another net, and rub extra soap all over with bubble wrap. Put the bubble wrap to one side once you have finished.

10 Place the dowel on the mat, and roll the mat up around it. Place a towel underneath the mat, and then roll firmly backwards and forwards fifteen times.

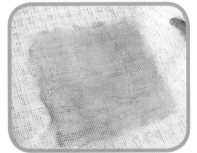

11 Unroll, and turn the net 'parcel' ninety degrees clockwise.

12 Roll the mat backwards and forwards fifteen times, then unroll, turn the parcel and repeat the process twice more.

13 Remove the nets to reveal your completed green pre-felt (see inset). Make more pre-felts in the following colours: light yellow, dark yellow, pink, purple and red. Use the sharp scissors to cut out these shapes: six pink star-shaped flowers with six light yellow dots for the centres; seven light yellow daffodils with large dark yellow dots for the trumpets; five red flowers with purple dots for the centres; twelve circular green leaves and six heart-shaped green leaves.

14 Remove the top net from the white merino background that was prepared earlier (see step 7). Begin to build up colour in the background sky by adding thin wisps of blue tops.

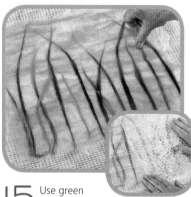

15 Use green tops to build up stems and grasses as shown, then cover the background with net, and massage all over with soapy bubble wrap (see inset).

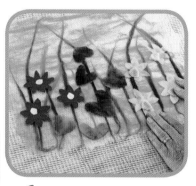

16 Remove the net, and place pre-felted shapes on the background as shown.

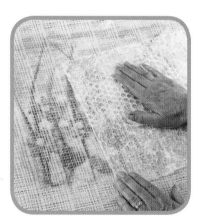

17 Cover the piece with net, and massage all over with soapy bubble wrap.

18 Turn the 'parcel' over, and remove the net to reveal the back of the piece.

19 Build up the surface design on the back in the same way.

20 Re-cover with net when complete, then begin felting as for pre-felts: roll the parcel back and forth fifteen times. Unroll. Turn it through 90 degrees and roll again. Continue until you have rolled from all four sides. Turn over and repeat rolling in the same way, with this side uppermost.

21 Remove the top net, and turn the work over. Lift off the second piece of net, replace the dowel and continue rolling the felt in the mat, turning as you go: first on one side, and then the other.

TOP TIP!

Open out the felt from time to time to check on progress. The fibres should start to lock together and stop moving around.

22 Turn the work over, and repeat the rolling and turning as before.

23 Continue rolling the felt around the mat in all directions. At the end of each round, turn the felt over and continue rolling until the fibres do not move when you rub the surface with your fingers (see inset).

24 Roll the felt firmly around the dowel (without the mat) in all directions. The piece will gradually tighten up and shrink. Work until it measures 23 x 30cm (9 x 12in).

25 Rinse out all the soap, and place in a vinegar rinse to neutralise (see inset).

26 Wrap the piece in a dry towel, and squeeze out the water by standing on the towel.

27 Pull the felt into shape, and iron with a hot iron on both sides until it is flat, then leave to dry completely. This completes the front cover of the book.

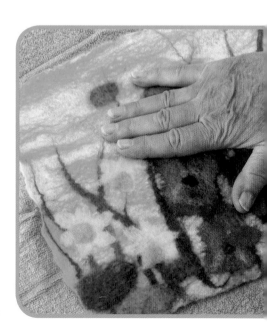

The completed front cover, and the other side (see inset).

28 Make another background sheet with white merino wool and add wisps of blue as before.

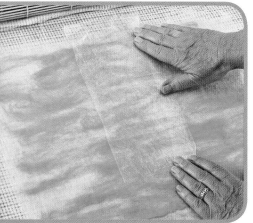

29 Place a piece of thin plastic in the centre of the sheet as shown, with one end extending beyond the top. This is a resist for the pocket.

30 Place two layers of wool on top so that the plastic is completely covered on three sides, with the top edge showing the rest of the plastic. This will stop the top edge of the pocket from felting into the background.

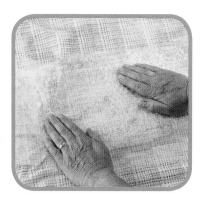

31 Sprinkle the pocket layers with soap solution and cover with a net. Rub extra soap on to bubble wrap and massage it into the background sheet.

32 Remove the net and build up the design on the surface, using the pre-felt flower shapes as shown. You can move the top part of the plastic to add pre-felts behind it (see inset). Make sure to put the plastic back in place before continuing.

33 Wet the piece with soap solution, cover it with the net and rub all over with the soaped bubble wrap.

34 Roll the dowel up in the mat, then begin rolling to felt the parcel as before. After four rounds of rolling (i.e. having turned it all the way round), turn the parcel over and repeat on the back.

35 Remove the nets and continue rolling and turning on both sides until nothing on the surface moves. Slide your fingers into the pocket formed by the plastic resist every so often to make sure it stays open (see inset).

36 Wrap the felt round the dowel, then roll in all directions. As you work, the plastic resist will work itself loose, so take it out (see inset).

TOP TIP!

After the plastic has been removed, slip your hand into the pocket occasionally as you work to make sure that it does not felt itself closed.

37 Knead the work on the mat until it is slightly smaller than the front cover. Rinse out the soap and place the work in the vinegar rinse. Remove it from the rinse and dry it in a towel. Pull it into shape and iron flat. Leave to dry.

38 Make a back cover in the same way as the front cover. You will need to cut out the following from your pre-felts: three pink star-shaped flowers with three light yellow dots for the centres; seven light yellow daffodils; eleven red flowers with purple dots for the centres; and eight purple bell-shaped flowers. The reverse of the back cover is shown in the inset.

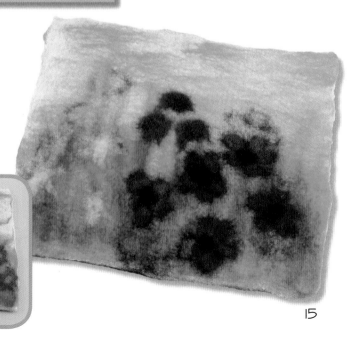

39 Layer the three pieces together as shown.

40 Thread a needle with turquoise cotton and take it up through all three felt layers from the back. Take the needle up through a button, then back through the button and the felt layers. Repeat several times then secure on the back.

41 Repeat with four more buttons to complete the Secret Garden book.

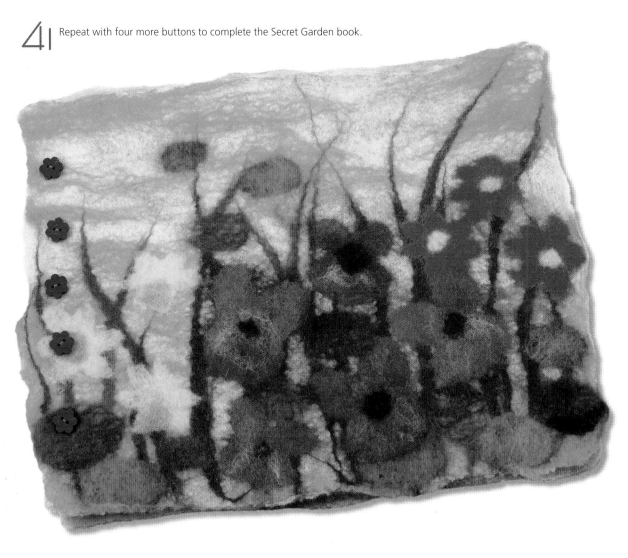

The finished Secret Garden book.

This Treasure Chest book uses the same techniques, but with an under-the-sea theme.

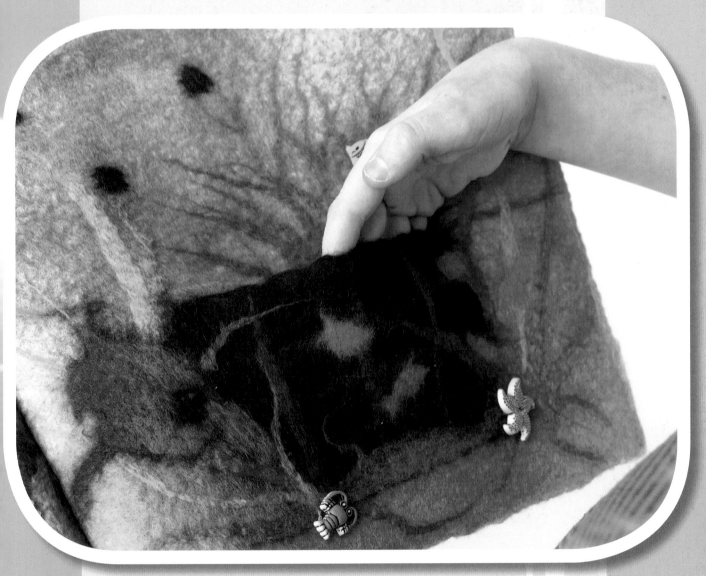

The pocket in the Treasure Chest book can be used to hold your secrets!

What next?

Using these flat felting methods, you can go on to make pictures or your own table mats – felt will protect the table from hot plates, and you could have pockets for your cutlery!

You could make scarf for yourself. Because this would be a little bigger, you would need to use a longer felting mat and longer nylon netting (sheers) for this. These mats usually measure two metres (78¾in) in length, and the nylon nets would also have to be the same length.

Lots more ideas, lots more magic, and lots more fun!

Book Bag

This project will introduce you to hollow wet felt rolling techniques, which are developed from the pocket-making used in the Secret Garden project (see pages 10–17). It also includes making a loop and a shoulder strap, which are felted into the bag for strength, and a button as a fastening.

You will need

Variegated green, blue, red, orange and yellow merino tops

Equipment for flat wet felting and hollow wet felt rolling (see page 8)

Glycerine soap

Vinegar rinse

Needle and thread

Measuring jug

Thick, flexible plastic

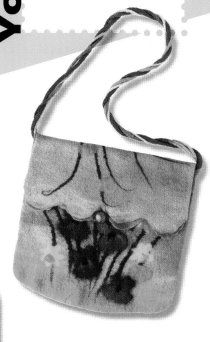

Pattern

The pattern for the book bag resist template, reproduced at one third of the actual size. You will need to photocopy this at 300 per cent for the correct size.

Make sure that the template is big enough to fit your book inside, allowing 5cm (2in) all round for shrinkage.

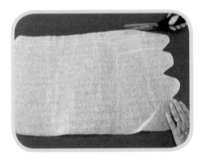

1 Transfer the pattern to thick, flexible plastic and cut it out with your scissors. Cut around the solid line first, then cut into the dotted line to make the shaped edge. This is your resist template.

2 Put a piece of clear plastic on the cane mat, and place the resist template on top with the shaped edge on the right as shown.

3 Wet both sides of the resist template and rub extra soap all over it. This will hold the woollen fibres in place.

4 Using various shades of green wool, lay out the first layer of wool tops on top of the resist in rows to form an even covering from edge to edge.

5 Sprinkle with the soap solution and cover with a piece of clear plastic.

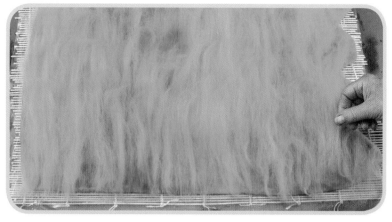

6 Turn the parcel over so the shaped edge is on the left and peel away the plastic. Take any wool that is lying beyond the edges and bring them over on to the resist template (see inset), then place a layer of green tops in the same direction as the first. Sprinkle with soap solution and replace the clear plastic.

7 Turn the parcel over so the shaped edge is on the right and remove the plastic. Bring the surplus wool over the edges as before, then lay the second layer of tops at right angles to the first.

8 Sprinkle the wool with the soap solution, then lay the clear plastic sheet over it once again. Turn it over.

9 Remove the clear plastic and bring the surplus wool over before laying the second layer of wool on this side in the opposite direction as shown.

10 Sprinkle with soap solution, cover with clear plastic, and turn over. Bring the surplus wool over, and put the piece to one side.

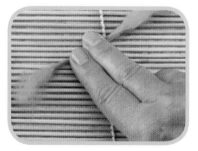

11 To make the loop for the button fastening, pull off a small amount of blue tops and wet the centre with soap solution. Make sure that you keep the ends dry.

12 Put your fingers on the wetted centre section, and roll the wool on the ridged mat until it is firm.

13 Place the button loop in the centre of the flap edge, pressing the dry ends into the wet wool.

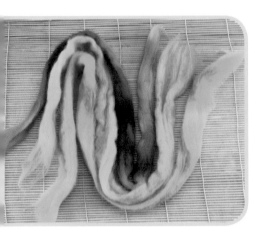

14 Divide a 1m (39¼in) length of blue tops into three equal lengths and put two aside. Repeat with green and red tops to get three narrow strips, each 1m (39¼in) long. These will make the strap.

TOP TiP!

Measure the length of the tops against your body to get the finished size for the strap. Allow 5cm (2in) for shrinkage.

15 Holding both ends of one length in one hand to keep them dry, dip the rest of the length in soap solution.

16 Rub extra soap into the wet section (see inset), and roll it on the mat with your hands until the strap is firm. Make sure that you keep the ends dry while you felt the centre.

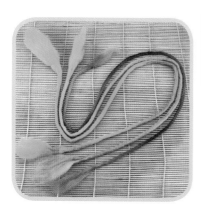

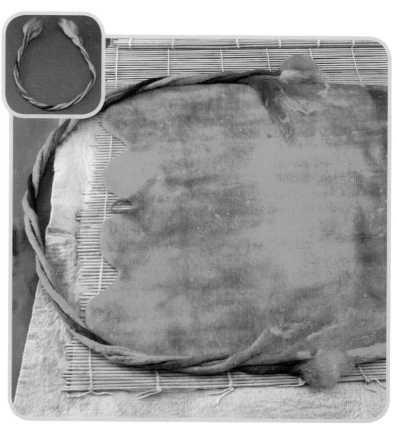

17 Repeat on the other two lengths and put them to one side for the moment.

18 Take the lengths of cord and twist them together (see inset), then place the dry ends where you would like the strap to be attached to the bag. Spread out and press the dry ends into the wet wool, leaving half of each of the dry tufts sticking out at the sides.

19 Cover the piece with plastic and turn over so the shaped edge is on the right, then remove the plastic on the back and press in the other half of the dry tufts as shown.

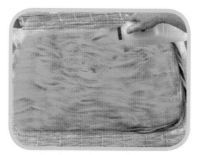

20 Using the blue tops, place the third layer of wool on the piece in the same direction as the first, and use soap solution to wet it.

21 Cover the piece with plastic and turn over, then bring the surplus wool over the edges as before and layer blue tops on this side. Wet with soap solution and cover with plastic sheeting.

22 Complete the fourth layer on both sides by laying the wool down in the opposite direction to the third layer, still using the blue tops.

23 Prepare yellow, light orange, dark orange, green and purple pre-felts (see pages 11–12 for the method of making pre-felts). Cut out the shapes shown: eight orange poppies with purple dots for the centres; six yellow daffodils with light orange trumpets; and ten green round leaves.

24 Remove the plastic from the piece, then use wisps of light and dark green tops to suggest grasses and stems as shown.

TOP TIP!

Add a wisp of a contrasting coloured top to the pre-felted shape to add interest to the surface.

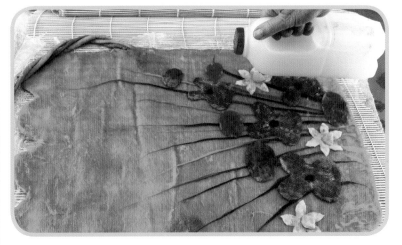

25 Use half of the pre-felted shapes to decorate the lower half of the bag as shown. Sprinkle with soap solution to wet the pre-felts to the surface.

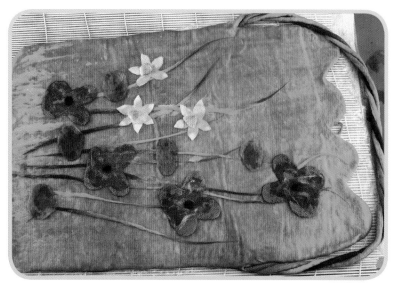

27 Cover with a nylon net (sheers) and rub extra soap over the surface. Press down with both hands from the outside edge towards the middle to secure the pre-felts in place and neaten the edges.

26 Cover the piece with plastic before turning over and decorate the entire other side of the bag as shown.

28 Turn the parcel over and remove the plastic sheet. Cover with another piece of nylon net, and rub extra soap all over before pressing inwards with your hands.

29 Roll up the parcel with the mat on to the dowel, and place a towel underneath to stop things sliding around. It will also soak up any surplus water that you do not need.

30 Roll the parcel backwards and forwards fifteen times. Turn through ninety degrees and roll again.

31 Repeat this rolling and turning process twice more on one side before turning over, and doing the same on the other side.

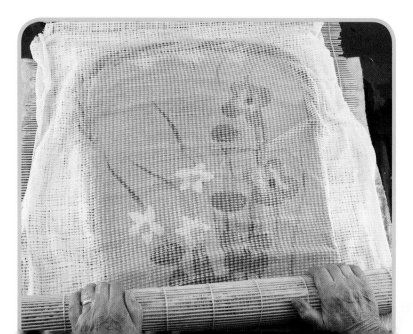

32 Repeat the whole process four more times on both sides, then remove the nylon nets.

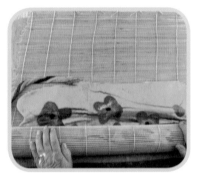

33 Continue rolling without the nets, until you notice that either it becomes difficult to roll, or the edges of the plastic resist are beginning to curl.

34 Using a sharp pair of scissors, cut along the edge of the flap opening.

TOP TIP!

Rub extra soap on to any flower shapes that are not sticking to the surface.

35 Remove the resist template and turn the bag inside out (see inset).

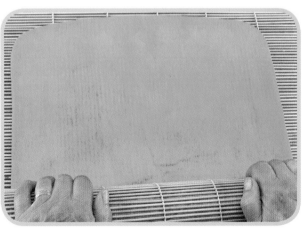

36 Continue to roll with the mat and the dowel in all directions on both sides, occasionally putting your hand inside to stop anything from felting together.

37 Once the inside has felted, turn the bag the right way out. Place the opening on the edge of the mat, and roll with the mat and dowel, for extra strength.

38 Open the bag, and move it round slightly before rolling it again. Continue doing this until you reach where you started.

39 Place the whole bag in the centre of the mat, and continue rolling in all directions until it reaches the size you want it to be. Fold the flap over from the back to the front as shown.

40 Rinse out all the soap in a basin of clean warm water.

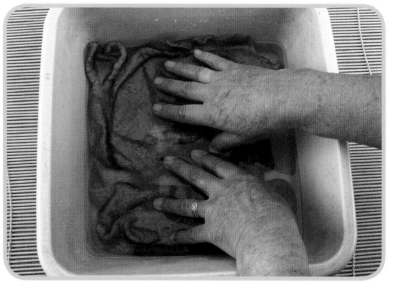

41 Place the bag in the vinegar rinse to neutralise the soap, then dry it in a towel.

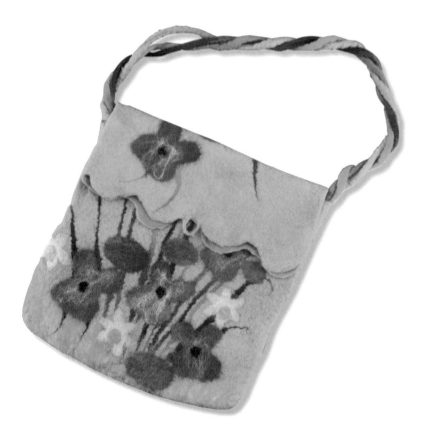

42 Press the bag with a hot iron until smooth. Put aside to dry.

43 Roll up some yellow and orange tops into a tight ball, and dip it in a basin of warm soapy water.

44 Rub extra soap on one hand, and gently roll the ball of wool so that it is covered with this soap. Do not squeeze the ball.

45 Roll the ball of wool gently in your hands until the fibres are holding together. Then roll more vigorously until you have a perfect sphere. This will be a button.

TOP TIP!

If the fibres begin to separate when you are rolling the ball, don't panic! Wrap some more wool tightly round the ball, wet it, soap it as before, then continue rolling.

46 Rinse out the soap in clean water, then wash the ball in vinegar rinse before drying it in a towel.

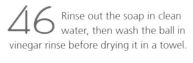

47 Finally, use the needle and thread to sew the button in place in the middle of the bag. Make sure that the button loop fits snugly over the ball.

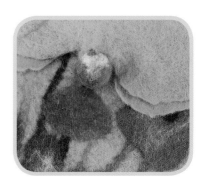

The finished
Book Bag

What next?

Using this method for making hollow felts, you can make mobile phone covers, purses, egg cosies, tea cosies and even a pair of mittens.

Making a resist template for the mittens by drawing round your hand, and add 5cm (2in) all the way round for shrinkage.

Felted Jewellery

Bracelets and necklaces can be made by stringing together felt beads. They can also be sewn on to hats and bags as decorations, and are a great way of using up oddments of leftover wool. The more colours you can use, the more exciting the results will be!

You will need

Pink, green, yellow, blue, purple, orange, red, turquoise and <u>random-dyed</u> merino tops

Equipment for flat wet rolling and 3D wet felting (see page 8)

Blue silk cord and a large-eyed needle

Sharp scissors

Necklace clasp jewellery findings

Clear glue

Metallic seed beads

Glycerine soap

Vinegar rinse

Bead Bracelet

Making felt beads is just like making the buttons on the Book Bag (see page 29).

1 Put some warm soapy water in a bowl, then roll up some pink and green tops into a tight ball. Dip the ball in the soap solution.

2 Lather some soap on your hand, and gently roll the ball of wool so that it is covered with the soap.

3 Wet a wisp of yellow tops and wrap it around the ball.

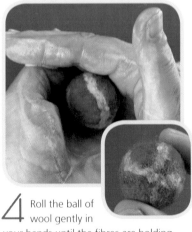

4 Roll the ball of wool gently in your hands until the fibres are holding together. Then gradually roll more vigorously until you have a perfect sphere (see inset).

5 Make five more round beads using different coloured tops for each, but always adding a yellow wisp.

6 Make a lozenge-shaped bead by rolling the felt bead backwards and forwards in your hands instead of round and round.

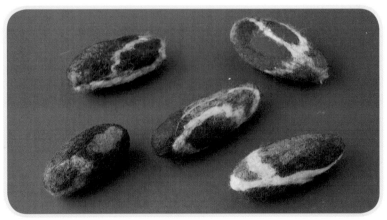

7 Make four more lozenge-shaped beads, again using different colours for each one, but adding a yellow wisp every time.

9 Dry all of the beads by wrapping them in a towel and squeezing out the water by standing on them.

8 Rinse the beads in clean warm water and then in a vinegar rinse.

33

10 Thread a needle with blue silk cord (see inset), then take the needle through the beads, alternating round and lozenge-shaped ones, until you have strung them all on to the thread.

TOP TIP!

If you find it hard to push the needle through a bead, use a pair of pliers to pull the needle through.

11 Take the silk cord through the loop of the clasp, then take it right over left and through itself as shown.

12 Take the cord left over right and through to make a knot.

13 Add a dab of clear glue to the knot to stop it coming undone.

14 When dry, use the scissors to trim the cord close to the knot, then repeat on the other end with the toggle end of the clasp.

Beaded Necklace

In this necklace, the beads are matching, and are made by slicing through a felted cylinder made from several layers of contrasting colours. Every time you cut a slice, it is a surprise!

1   Lay a handful of turquoise tops running across the ridged mat.

2   Put a layer of red tops on top of the turquoise tops at a ninety degree angle to the previous layer.

3   Continue adding layers in contrasting colours, alternating the directions until you have six layers.

4   Place a line of blue tops along one edge.

5   Roll the wool up tightly into a cylinder.

6   Hold the cylinder in both hands and dip it in a bowl of soap solution until it is thoroughly wet all the way through.

7   Place it on the mat and gently rub extra soap over the surface.

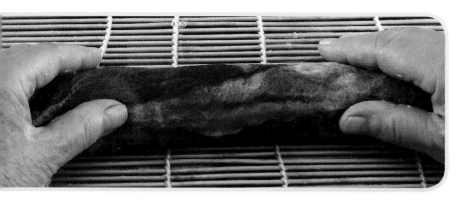

8 Carefully roll the cylinder back and forth on the mat until the fibres begin to hold together. The ends will begin to take on a pointed shape.

9 Continue rolling more and more vigorously to felt the piece into a shape that does not bend when you hold it up.

10 Rinse out the soap in clean water, then rinse the shape in a vinegar rinse before drying it in a towel.

11 Cut off both of the ends and put them to one side. These will be the toggles for the necklace.

12 Use a sharp pair of scissors to cut into the cylinder at an angle (see inset), and cut it into seventeen beads as shown.

13 Thread a needle with 75cm (29½in) of blue silk cord. Knot the end and take it up through the point of one of the toggles and out of the top as shown.

14 Take the needle back down through the toggle and out through the point. Pull the cord through until the knot catches at the point.

15 Thread the beads on to the cord one by one by taking the needle through one side and out of the other. Leave 15cm (6in) of cord between the toggle and the first bead.

16 Leave 15cm (6in) of cord after the final bead, then attach the second toggle in the same way as the first to complete the necklace.

Cord Bracelet

This is a development from the cords used for making the strap in the Book Bag project (see pages 20–29), and can be used in many different ways. For added interest, I have used random-dyed merino tops.

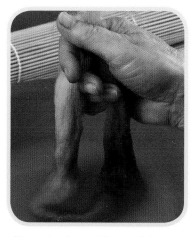

1 Pull off a 40cm (15¾in) length of random-dyed tops and divide it into three equal parts.

2 Make a loop with one of the lengths and dip it in the soap solution, keeping the ends dry.

3 Add extra soap to your hand and run it over the wet loop.

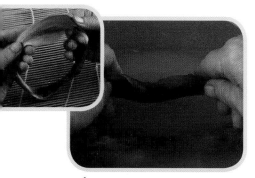

4 Put the dry ends together to make a hoop (see inset), then dip the dry part into the soap solution, holding it firmly together.

5 Soap your hand and work the soap into the join, rolling in short back-and-forth motions on the mat to begin to felt the bracelet.

6 Work all the way round the bracelet in small sections to felt the cord until firm.

7 Work the other two lengths in the same way and put them on your wrist to ensure they fit and are all the same size.

8 Wrap an 18cm (7in) piece of purple tops around all three cords.

9 Dip the purple tops wrap in the soap solution. This will form a link to hold the cords together.

10 Soap the purple link and rub it between your hands to felt it.

11 As you felt the link, push it together occasionally to prevent the wool from spreading sideways.

12 Once it is firm, add another two links to the cords. Rinse in clean water, then vinegar rinse. Dry the bracelet in a towel.

13 Thread a needle with blue silk cord. Take it through the link and round to secure it. Thread a bead on to the needle.

14 Take the needle through the link, pick up another bead and take it through the link again as shown. Repeat.

15 Repeat until the link is covered in beads. Secure the thread by making two stitches in the same place. Take the needle through the link once more so that the thread comes out in a different place, and trim off the excess.

16 Decorate the other links in the same way to finish the bracelet.

The finished Felted Jewellery.

What next?

The ideas here show how the design can easily be changed.

You can join lozenge-shaped beads together to make bead bracelets, and sewing on glass beads adds a touch of sparkle.

Cord necklaces can be made with open ends and joined together with an adjustable toggle, made in the same way as the links on the Cord Bracelet (see pages 38–39).

Fine cords can be felted on to hair bands, and mini cord bands can become rings on fingers! There are lots of possibilities – have fun!

Charms

Here is a simple way of creating miniature sculptures that you can add to any of your projects, or use as a decoration on a felted cord to make an unusual necklace.

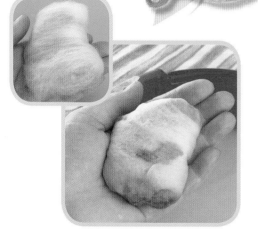

1 Wrap the stone tightly with a small amount of yellow tops (see inset), and dip thoroughly in a bowl of warm soapy water.

2 Soap a hand and rub the lather gently over the wetted wool.

TOP TIP!

Remember the merino wool will shrink to half its original size in this project, so make sure the stone you use is not too small to start with.

3 Add more wool a little at a time until the whole stone is covered, wetting and soaping after each addition.

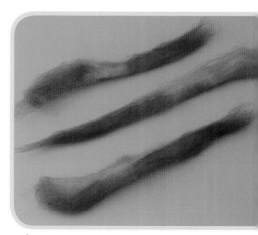

4 Take three 30cm (12in) lengths of red tops.

5 Fold one of the lengths in half and dip into soap solution. Do not wet it all the way, but leave 7.5cm (3in) or so dry.

6 Rub more soap into the length, being careful to keep the tuft at the end dry.

7 Roll the length on the mat as shown to felt the wet part into a point.

8 Repeat the process with the other two lengths so you have three points.

9 Open up one of the dry tufts and place it on the wet stone as shown.

10 Wrap a small amount of yellow tops tightly around the whole rock, covering the dry ends of the tuft.

11 Repeat with the other two points, securing them in place with yellow tops. Make sure that the stone remains wet – add more soap solution if necessary.

12 Take a new 30cm (12in) length of red tops and make a loop. Dip the centre in soap solution, making sure that both ends stay dry.

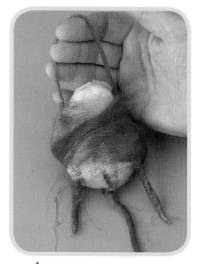

13 Roll the wet part on the mat to felt it into a cord, making sure to keep the tufts on both ends dry.

14 Use the dry tufts to attach it in a loop to the wet stone, then use red tops to secure and cover the tufts.

15 Dip the whole charm in soap solution, then rub in extra soap as you begin to wrap red tops around the charm.

16 Continue wrapping red tops and wetting the charm with soap solution until the yellow is completely covered.

17 Take a short length of multi-coloured tops and wet it with soap solution. Place it in a spiral design on the charm.

18 Wrap the charm in the plastic netting and rub the charm through the net to felt it. Add extra soap as you work.

19 When you can rub the spiral design without it lifting off, remove the netting and continue rubbing the whole charm to felt it firmly.

20 Continue rubbing the charm gently until there is no movement on the surface of the stone.

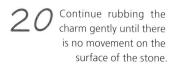

21 Use a pair of sharp-pointed scissors to cut a slit in the felt between the places where the loop is attached to the charm. Cut across the slit to make a cross-shaped opening.

22 Extend the slit until you can remove the stone.

23 Re-wet the charm and add soap all over it, both inside and out.

24 Rub the inside of the charm with your fingers to felt it.

25 Rub the inside of the charm over the mat to shape it as you continue felting the piece, turning it round as you go.

26 Rinse the charm thoroughly in clean water.

27 Wash the charm in vinegar rinse to neutralise the wool.

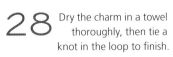

28 Dry the charm in a towel thoroughly, then tie a knot in the loop to finish.

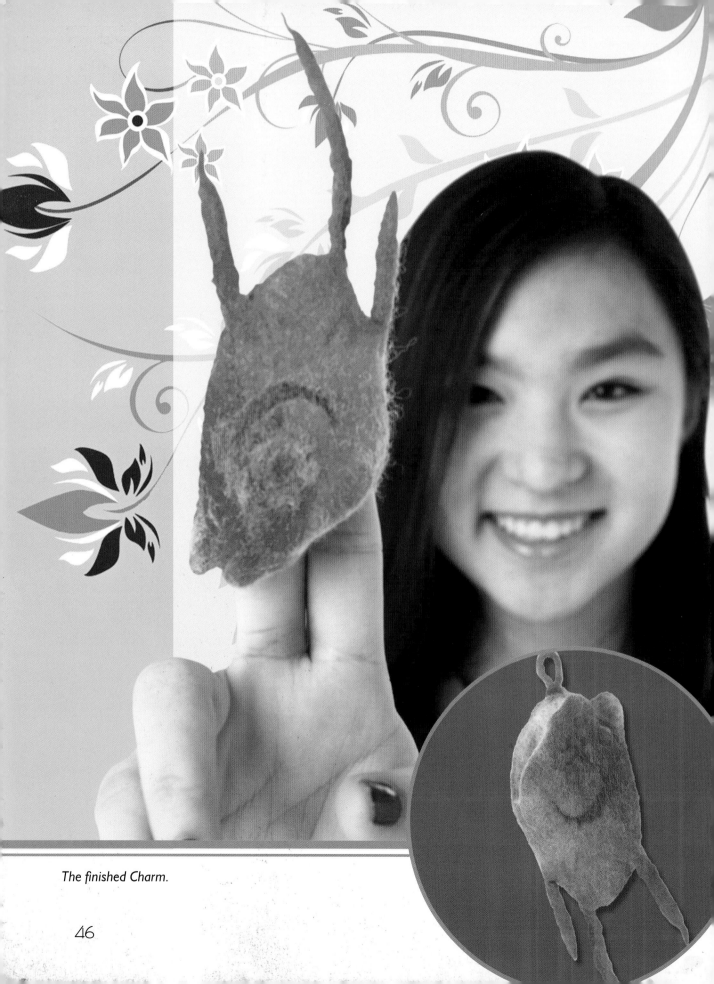

The finished Charm.

What next?

The ideas here show how the design can easily be changed.
Remember that the shape of the stone you use will
determine the size and final shape of your charm.
Jazz up the surface by sewing beads on, or attach the charm
to a felted cord to make a necklace.
Alternatively, place a precious stone or keepsake inside, or
simply leave the stone inside and use it as a paperweight!

More books to read

Felt in the Kitchen by Ewa Kuniczak, Felt Head to Toe, 2001
More Felt in the Kitchen by Ewa Kuniczak, Felt Head to Toe, 2002
Yet More Felt in the Kitchen by Ewa Kuniczak, Felt Head to Toe, 2002

Useful websites

www.feltheadtotoe.co.uk; www.winghamwoolwork.co.uk;
www.blacksheepdesigns.com; www.feltmakers.com

Glossary

This list explains the meaning of some of the more unusual words in this book.
Bradford count The measurement of wool fibre in UK, related to its
spinning length.
Dowel or **dowelling** Tube-shaped wood.
Findings Jewellery fittings.
Lanolin Natural oil found in unwashed sheep's wool.
Merino Type of sheep bred in Australia and New Zealand. The wool fibres are
long and crimped (curly), which helps them tangle together easily.
Micron Measurement of fibre size outside the UK, based on the diameter
of the fibre.
Pre-felts Slightly felted wool.
Random-dyed Several colours are deliberately spread unevenly during the dyeing.
Tops Industrially washed and combed fibres that lie in the same direction, and are bought
in lengths, called hanks or slivers.
Vinegar rinse Vinegar contains four per cent acetic acid, which neutralises any alkaline
soap left in the felt. This stops it from rotting over time. Mix two tablespoons of distilled
vinegar with one litre (two US pints) of water to make vinegar rinse.

Index

3D wet felting 8, 32

bag 20, 21, 23, 24, 25, 26, 28, 29, 30, 32
beads 7, 32, 33, 34, 35, 36, 37, 39, 41, 47
bracelet 7, 32, 38, 39, 41
book 10, 13, 16, 17, 18, 30
button 7, 10, 16, 20, 22, 29, 32

charm 42, 44, 45

mat 8, 10, 11, 19, 21, 22, 28, 35, 36, 38, 43, 44, 45
flat wet rolling 8, 10, 20, 32, 42
hollow wet felt rolling 8, 20, 42

merino wool 6, 10, 12, 20, 32, 42

necklace 7, 32, 35, 36, 37, 41, 42, 47
needle and thread 7, 10, 16, 20, 29, 32, 34, 37, 39, 42
nylon netting (sheers) 8, 10, 11, 12, 13, 15, 19, 26, 27

plastic resist 8, 10, 14, 15, 20, 21, 22, 27, 30
plastic sheeting 8, 22, 24, 26
pocket 10, 14, 15
pre-felts 10, 11, 12, 13, 14, 15, 25, 26

rolling 13, 15, 26, 27, 28, 38

soap 6, 7, 8, 9, 10, 11, 13, 14, 15, 20, 21, 23, 26, 29, 32, 35, 42, 43, 44, 45
soap solution 7, 15, 21, 22, 23, 24, 25, 28, 35, 36, 38, 39, 43, 44
stone 7, 42, 43, 44, 45

tops 6, 10, 12, 20, 21, 22, 23, 24, 25, 29, 32, 35, 38, 39, 42, 43, 44
towel 8, 13, 28, 29, 33, 36, 39, 45

vinegar rinse 7, 9, 10, 13, 15, 20, 28, 29, 32, 33, 36, 39, 42, 45

wool 6, 8, 10, 14, 22, 24, 25, 29, 32, 33, 35, 42, 45